Contents

I. Jump-Start the Action: Openers, Icebreakers, and Mixers

II. Build Strengths Together: Team-Building Exercises and Games

III. Go Deeper with Assets: Asset-Building Mind Benders and Brain Teasers

IV. Games for Youth and Adults: Intergenerational Activities

V. Wrap Things Up: Closers and Reflections

Acknowledgments

This resource would not have been possible without the contributions of some very talented and inspiring asset builders across the country.

Special thanks to Karen Atkinson, Tim Duffey, Emily Foster, Rebecca Grothe, Merry Klemme, Nancy Leyerzapf, Shirley Luce, Marilyn Peplau, Derek Peterson, Clay Roberts, Cynthia Sosnowski, and Jim Williams. Their wonderful ideas and activities fill the pages of this publication.

Also special thanks to the editors and other staff members at Search Institute who contributed their time and talents to the shaping of this resource: Shelby Andress, Jennifer Griffin-Wiesner, Kay Hong, Kathleen Kimball-Baker, Becky Manfredini, Gene Roehlkepartain, Terri Sullivan, and Nancy Tellet-Royce. Building assets in communities is a tireless effort that all of us share and believe in. Together we can and will continue to improve the lives of youth!

Introduction: It Starts with You!

Meetings, meetings, meetings! Whether you're a student, teacher, youth worker, administrator, or community leader, it probably seems like there are dozens of meetings that you are expected to arrange, facilitate, attend, or decline.

For asset builders in communities across the nation, meetings play an important role in distributing information about the 40 developmental assets to the people who are curious or waiting to be convinced. People have the opportunity to share their knowledge, learn from the experiences of others, and gain from the momentum that builds when people with common interests and goals come together. Meetings are also great opportunities to get people excited about what they can do individually and collectively to build assets for youth. The challenge that many presenters, facilitators, and coordinators face is making meetings interesting and fun, as well as informative and productive.

Get Things Going! is a resource designed to give youth and adult presenters fun and practical asset-building activities and games that can be easily incorporated into presentations and meetings. Presenters can use these tools to connect the assets message to adults and youth in their own communities. Workshops, conferences, retreats, and neighborhood gatherings are all settings in which the ideas in this book would be appropriate.

We've heard from asset builders across the country that stronger communities and healthier youth often begin with the efforts of one or two creative people who can imagine the possibilities. It can start with you and this publication gives some great ideas to get you going.

How This Book Is Organized

The activities featured in this book all target issues related to the developmental asset framework developed by Search Institute. Each activity description includes a list of materials, suggested group sizes, and time estimates. Also included with each activity are asset-building teaching points that can serve as conversation starters or key messages to highlight.

Many of the activities and games you will find in this book came from people in the field who are working very hard to connect asset building to their communities. In those cases the names and their community are listed.

To help you decide which activities are right for your setting, they are divided into five sections:

Jump-Start the Action—This is a collection of icebreakers and mixers that will help groups get acquainted with each other and set the tone for your time together.

Build Strengths Together—Here you will find a variety of team-building activities to encourage groups to collectively problem solve and brainstorm.

Go Deeper with Assets—This section features activities that focus specifically on increasing participants' knowledge and understanding of the 40 assets.

Games for Youth and Adults—Children, youth, and adults can learn and participate together in these activities that target intergenerational themes and audiences.

Wrap Things Up—These activities will help bring closure to the ideas and thoughts expressed during the meeting, help participants reflect on materials and information presented, and spark enthusiasm for continued involvement with asset building.

How Can You Use These Activities and Games?

Activities and games can play an important role in the connection a presenter can have with her or his audiences. Here are some ways in which games and activities can be an effective part of your meeting or presentation.

• *Games and activities can help participants feel that they are part of a group.* Participants have the opportunity to share past experiences including challenges and triumphs and, if only for a short time, an increased sense of belonging.

• *Games and activities break down barriers between generations.* Accomplishing a common task together can help adults see young people as resources.

• *Games and activities provide a learning situation that is a new experience for all participants and creates a common point of reference.* These situations can lead to a sense of "equal footing" in a community setting and give everyone a sense of empowerment.

• *Games and activities enhance motivation to stay "tuned in to" the speaker.* What better way to connect with your audience than with something in which everyone present can be involved?

• *Games and activities reinforce the idea that learning is fun.*

Why is it a good idea to use games and activities?

Games and activities are helpful for:
• Providing duplication and repetition in enjoyable ways;
• Enhancing the experience for those who are kinesthetic learners;
• Engaging more senses in learning; and
• Strengthening existing associations for learning and building new ones.

When might you use a game or activity?

Games and activities are great for situations like the following:
• As icebreakers when you have a group of people who don't know each other well or at all;
• When you want to incorporate active learning (always a good idea);
• When you need to illustrate a concept or theory; and
• To close a meeting, summarize, and call to action.

Pearls of Wisdom from the Field:
Leading Effective Asset-Building Presentations and Meetings

In addition to including games and activities in presentations or meetings, there are a number of steps you can take to help ensure that you connect with your audience, that they understand the information, and that they are motivated to take action.

Marilyn Peplau, team member of the Healthy Communities • Healthy Youth (HC • HY) initiative in New Richmond, Wisconsin, and Derek Peterson, director of child and youth advocacy for the Association of Alaska School Boards in Anchorage, Alaska, are two pioneers in the asset-building movement. Based on years of experience, they offer the following suggestions to keep in mind when holding meetings and making asset-building presentations to people in your community.

• When you first walk into the room, introduce yourself to at least one person you don't know. Shake her or his hand, look in her or his eyes, remember the person's name, and listen to what he or she has to say. You can then call upon this person later, if you need to.

• Your presentation will be most effective if you reach the hearts, souls, and minds of the participants. Feelings and values motivate people. Not all people are motivated by logic, but for most, it is important to know that the information is sound and credible. The assets framework is so powerful because it can appeal to the hearts, souls, and minds of participants.

• Remember to be sensitive to the needs of the group and try to accommodate those needs as often as possible. Some activities (particularly in this publication) require participants to stand, move around the room, and do other tasks. Not everyone will be able to do these things. It's the responsibility of the presenter to recognize this, adapt, and find ways to include everyone.

• Some activities and games ask participants to recall past experiences (e.g., in childhood, with family or friends). Keep in mind that some of these memories may not always be pleasant for participants. A positive attitude and willingness to keep the focus of the activity positive will help the facilitator and the group.

• To make the most of planned games or activities during a meeting or presentation, it's important for presenters to keep certain things in mind. Know the goal for the game or activity you plan to use. Choose appropriately, keeping in mind space and time constraints. Prepare the setup ahead of time and gather all needed materials. Craft the transitions into and out of the game to make the experience more meaningful to participants. Ask good discussion questions that allow participants to learn. Last of all, watch the clock!

• Effective games and activities have the following characteristics: they are short, adaptable, and enjoyable; may use simple and inexpensive props; supplement the main purpose or content of the meeting or presentation; and encourage group participation.

• Encourage people to ask questions as often as they need to. All of us have wondered about youth, our role as caring adults and/or youth, boundaries, expectations, and other issues. One strategy for generating questions is to encourage participants at the beginning of the presentation to write on an index card a question that they have always wanted to ask related to children or youth. Such questions may address ideas for connecting with young people one-on-one, involving young people in board meetings, getting teens involved in asset building with younger children, or making intergenerational activities successful. Participants then form pairs, introduce themselves, and answer each other's questions. You can ask people to switch partners as many times as your agenda allows.

• For groups or teams that meet on a regular basis, an opening ritual, such as sharing joys and challenges, can unify the group, provide needed support, and set a positive and healthy tone to the meeting. Youth in particular seem comfortable with calling this type of opening ritual time "Brags and Bummers."

• When presenting the asset framework to specific groups in the community, celebrate their special gifts and connect the assets to their contributions. For example, if food service personnel are the participants and they are noted for their delicious bread, relate asset building to the task of baking bread. (Baking bread takes time and patience; if the process of ingredient mixing is interrupted it can do serious damage to the bread; it's important to mix the ingredients in the right environment.) This activity empowers people by connecting asset building to important parts of their daily work. And you'll be sure to leave a lasting impression: they'll always think about assets when they're performing their tasks.

• It has been said that people need to hear a message at least five times before they "get it." Therefore, it's a good idea to repeat your most important information several times. People learn in different ways, including repetition; keep in mind the different ways that you can communicate your message to others (e.g., music, visuals, brain teasers) and have a variety of activities for participants to be involved in.

• Ongoing groups or gatherings can celebrate asset building by naming individuals, organizations, and events that they have recently witnessed doing great things for children and youth. As a group, identify the assets that are being built by these individuals. Recognize those accomplishments by sending congratulatory certificates, notes, letters, or cards.

Well, now that we've gone through the preliminaries and got you thinking about the possibilities, it's time to get things going. Good luck!

What Are Developmental Assets?

Search Institute has identified 40 building blocks of development that help young people grow up healthy, caring, and responsible. The more of these developmental assets young people in a community say they have, the more likely they are to be leaders in their communities, succeed in school, resist danger, maintain good health, and overcome trouble. Youth who say they have assets are also less likely to abuse drugs, skip school, fight, or attempt suicide.

External Assets

Support

1. **Family support**—Family life provides high levels of love and support.
2. **Positive family communication**—Young person and her or his parent(s) communicate positively, and young person is willing to seek advice and counsel from parents.
3. **Other adult relationships**—Young person receives support from three or more nonparent adults.
4. **Caring neighborhood**—Young person experiences caring neighbors.
5. **Caring school climate**—School provides a caring, encouraging environment.
6. **Parent involvement in schooling**—Parent(s) are actively involved in helping young person succeed in school.

Empowerment

7. **Community values youth**—Young person perceives that adults in the community value youth.
8. **Youth as resources**—Young people are given useful roles in the community.
9. **Service to others**—Young person serves in the community one hour or more per week.
10. **Safety**—Young person feels safe at home, at school, and in the neighborhood.

Boundaries and Expectations

11. **Family boundaries**—Family has clear rules and consequences and monitors the young person's whereabouts.
12. **School boundaries**—School provides clear rules and consequences.
13. **Neighborhood boundaries**—Neighbors take responsibility for monitoring young people's behavior.
14. **Adult role models**—Parent(s) and other adults model positive, responsible behavior.
15. **Positive peer influence**—Young person's best friends model responsible behavior.
16. **High expectations**—Both parent(s) and teachers encourage the young person to do well.

Constructive Use of Time

17. **Creative activities**—Young person spends three or more hours per week in lessons or practice in music, theater, or other arts.
18. **Youth programs**—Young person spends three or more hours per week in sports, clubs, or organizations at school and/or in the community.
19. **Religious community**—Young person spends one or more hours per week in activities in a religious institution.
20. **Time at home**—Young person is out with friends "with nothing special to do" two or fewer nights per week.

Internal Assets

Commitment to Learning

21. **Achievement motivation**—Young person is motivated to do well in school.

22. **School engagement**—Young person is actively engaged in learning.

23. **Homework**—Young person reports doing at least one hour of homework every school day.

24. **Bonding to school**—Young person cares about her or his school.

25. **Reading for pleasure**—Young person reads for pleasure three or more hours per week.

Positive Values

26. **Caring**—Young person places high value on helping other people.

27. **Equality and social justice**—Young person places high value on promoting equality and reducing hunger and poverty.

28. **Integrity**—Young person acts on convictions and stands up for her or his beliefs.

29. **Honesty**—Young person "tells the truth even when it is not easy."

30. **Responsibility**—Young person accepts and takes personal responsibility.

31. **Restraint**—Young person believes it is important not to be sexually active or to use alcohol or other drugs.

Social Competencies

32. **Planning and decision making**—Young person knows how to plan ahead and make choices.

33. **Interpersonal competence**—Young person has empathy, sensitivity, and friendship skills.

34. **Cultural competence**—Young person has knowledge of and comfort with people of different cultural/racial/ethnic backgrounds.

35. **Resistance skills**—Young person can resist negative peer pressure and dangerous situations.

36. **Peaceful conflict resolution**—Young person seeks to resolve conflict nonviolently.

Positive Identity

37. **Personal power**—Young person feels he or she has control over "things that happen to me."

38. **Self-esteem**—Young person reports having a high self–esteem.

39. **Sense of purpose**—Young person reports that "my life has a purpose."

40. **Positive view of personal future**—Young person is optimistic about her or his personal future.

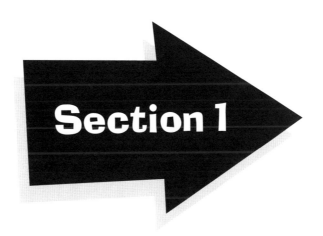

Section 1

Jump-Start the Action:

Openers, Icebreakers, and Mixers

#1 ▶ Asset Bingo Mixer

Purpose: To help participants learn one another's names and to think about their roles as asset builders.

Suggested Group Size: 12 to 100.

Estimated Time: 12 to 15 minutes.

Materials Needed: Asset Bingo sheet from page 4 (one for each person); pens; six or eight small prizes (such as a refrigerator magnet or candy bar).

Directions

1. Divide into teams of 4 to 8 people. Have the entire group play Asset Bingo—collecting signatures of individuals who fit the description in each box. The goal for participants is to fill a row, column, or diagonal completely. If the group is large enough, specify that each person should only sign the sheet once. Allow about 5 minutes.

2. Reconvene the small teams to count the total number of signatures for their group. Award the winning team members a small prize. If groups are not of equal size, have teams figure out the average number of signatures per team member.

Asset-Building Teaching Points

This is a good lead into reviewing the assets. ("We've all received assets from important people in our lives. And clearly, from all the signatures collected, people in this room are building assets! Let's refresh our memories about assets and their power . . .")

Tips for Success

Make sure the room you're using is large enough to allow comfortable mingling.

Variation

For smaller groups (under 20) ask individuals to provide names or titles of people who have built the assets listed in each box, asking them, "Who did this for you? or who are you doing this for?" Then ask participants to mingle until someone has a complete row, column, or diagonal. The winner will shout out "Forty Assets!" Then invite participants to discuss their own asset-building experiences.

40 Assets Bingo

(Each square represents one of the 40 developmental assets identified by Search Institute.)

Has returned money when got incorrect change at a store #29 Honesty	Has stood up to pressure to do something unhealthy #35 Resistance skills	FREE!	Has intervened when someone does something wrong in the neighborhood #13 Neighborhood boundaries	Is good at finding solutions when problems arise #37 Personal power	Has rarely felt bored in school #22 School engagement	Often volunteers to serve others #9 Service to others
Spent yesterday evening at home with family #20 Time at home	FREE!	Doesn't believe, "If it feels good, do it" #31 Restraint	Has/had teachers who encouraged to always do her or his best #16 High expectations	FREE!	Remembers people's birthdays #33 Interpersonal competence	Has rules about telling other family members where you are #11 Family boundaries
Is in the middle of a good book. (What is it?) #25 Reading for pleasure	Has role models who spend time helping others #14 Adult role models	Considers him or herself an optimist (why?) #40 Positive view of personal future	Eats dinner family most evenings #1 Family support	Has been laughed at for taking an unpopular stand on an issue #28 Integrity	Has a regular family meeting at home #2 Positive family communication	FREE!
Can't think of anyone else he/she would rather be #38 Self-esteem	Works hard to do best at school or work #21 Achievement motivation	FREE!	Has risen to a challenge because of encouragement from friends #15 Positive peer influence	Participated in religious activities during the past week #19 Religious community	Has made a major life choice because of a sense of purpose #39 Sense of purpose	Thanks young people when they take leadership #7 Community values youth
FREE!	Knows the school policy on violence/ bullying #12 School boundaries	Remembers an adult who really influenced his or her life (how?) #3 Other adult relationships	FREE!	Volunteers (or her/his parent volunteers) in a school #6 Parent involvement in school	Knows the school's cheer or fight song #24 Bonding to school	Knows names of at least 10 neighbors #4 Caring neighborhood
Participates or volunteers in a community youth program #18 Youth programs	Has worked hard to meet a commitment that wasn't enjoyable #30 Responsibility	Does or has done homework every school night #23 Homework	Does something unique to keep safe #10 Safety	Is fluent in two or more languages #34 Cultural competence	FREE!	Enjoys planning big projects #32 Planning and decision making
Did or does something to make a school more friendly #5 Caring school climate	Has training in conflict resolution #36 Peaceful conflict resolution	FREE!	Has been in a protest march to address a social issue or concern #27 Equality and social justice	Has helped find leadership opportunities #8 Youth as resources	Plays a musical instrument (which one?) #17 Creative activities	Raises or gives money to help with famine or disaster relief #26 Caring

#2 ▶ Candy Mixer

Purpose: To help participants learn one another's names and get to know a little bit about one another.

Suggested Group Size: 8 to 40.

Estimated Time: 15 minutes.

Materials Needed: One clear plastic cup for each person filled one-quarter with multicolored small candies; small plastic spoon for each person.

Directions

1. Give each participant a cup of candy and a spoon, telling them that they are not to eat the candy yet.

2. Ask participants to mingle, explaining that they cannot eat their candy until all their pieces are the same color. Participants will accomplish this by exchanging the candies with each other (using their spoons), but only after they say their names and answer one question. Presenters can tailor the questions to fit the setting. Ask participants to answer questions such as the following:

- What do you like to do in your spare time?

- What book have you read recently?

- What adult outside your family was most important to you when you were younger?

- What is one way you build assets in young people?

- Why did you come to this meeting/ presentation?

3. End the game by giving participants time to eat the candy.

Asset-Building Teaching Points

Asset building starts by building relationships, and building relationships starts with learning more about one another. A new relationship can begin with a conversation about a few simple questions.

Tips for Success

It's a good idea to prepare cups of candy before you begin this activity. You may also want to post potential questions for participants to see. An overhead transparency or flip chart pad works well. Instead of candy, you may want to exchange stickers in various colors or shapes or small pieces of paper in different colors.

Variations

Ask participants to exchange pieces of candy as fast as they can, without asking any questions. Then play the game as described. Talk about the differences: Which approach is more like how we live in our communities? Which one was more enjoyable? Why? What do the differences say about how we build relationships?

Or build asset #34: cultural competence. Start participants with all the same color candies in a cup and ask them to trade with each other to get a variety of colors. Then follow up with a discussion about the importance of diversity in communities.

#3 ▶ Valuable Objects

Purpose: To get participants thinking about how valuable young people are in our communities.

Suggested Group Size: At least 4.

Estimated Time: 5 minutes.

Materials Needed: A variety of simple objects, such as notepads, pencils, business cards, folders, envelopes, and/or chairs scattered throughout the room. Each team of 4 participants should have one to two pages of writing paper and a pencil or pen.

Directions

1. Divide your group into teams of about four. Ask each team to select a personal item that someone brought to the presentation or an item located somewhere in the room. Each group will use one item.

2. Ask each team to list the characteristics of its object—its positive features and how it might be useful, as well as traits that limit its value. Encourage team members to think creatively of uses that may not be typically associated with the item. Urge them to "think outside the box." For example, a business card can be cut into the shape of a boomerang that could be used around the office as a stress reliever.

3. Ask each team to report their conclusions back to the larger setting.

Asset-Building Teaching Points

Now that we've decided the value of these objects, think about the value of our young people. What would happen if we only considered the limitations of each of these objects? Would some of the ways in which we described the limitations of our designated objects be similar to the way in which we talk about what limits our youth? What about the positive descriptions? As asset builders, we need to be working toward finding ways to reinforce the positive characteristics of our young people. Certainly, if a simple object can be described as valuable, positive, and useful, we should be able to value our youth in the same way. Your creative new ideas for the object you described should remind us of the new possibilities for engaging our young people that are available if we are open to looking for them.

Tips for Success

This should be a fairly short activity. Giving teams more than about three or four minutes to list characteristics may lead them to get off the topic. This activity could have the potential to turn negative, so be sure to make an effort to keep the conversation positive.

Variations

After the teams have analyzed their objects, ask each team to pass its object to another team. Ask that team to go through the same exercise. Then ask the two teams to compare their conclusions. What do the two comparisons have in common? How are they different? Were there any insights in one group that enlightened another? Or if you want to make the point of new possibilities, you may only ask the group to generate lists of "nontypical" uses of the item they are describing.

Activity contributed by Marilyn Peplau, New Richmond, Wisconsin.

#4 ➤ Asset-Building Grand Pandemonium

Purpose: To give participants an opportunity to find out a few things about each other and to start the meeting on a high energy level.

Suggested Group Size: At least 12.

Estimated Time: 12 minutes.

Materials Needed: One copy of the Asset-Building Grand Pandemonium sheet from page 8 for each participant; pencils or pens; a bell, chime, or a way to blink the lights to signal time (avoid whistles; they remind many people of negative school experiences).

Directions

1. Distribute an Asset-Building Grand Pandemonium sheet facedown to each participant, asking them not to read their sheets until you have distributed them all.

2. Ask participants to turn the sheets over and read them. Explain that they will have 10 minutes to follow the instructions on the sheet and that you will signal when it is time to return to their seats.

3. Ask participants to try not to use the same person as a resource more than once.

4. Signal the end of the activity in 10 minutes.

5. Ask for a show of hands of people who completed their task (filled in all the blanks). Ask for a show of hands for those who did not. Ask for a show of hands for those who didn't and are upset about that.

Asset-Building Teaching Point

Process activity in a lighthearted way to point out that it can be okay not to "finish" some tasks; learning is often in the experience and not the final product.

Tips for Success

This activity requires enough space for participants to circulate and chat. It is not appropriate for theater-style seating. Pay attention to the activity and energy level of the group. Be prepared to end the activity if energy levels drop or if group members move off the task of meeting new people. Also, have extra copies of the sheet available for people to take with them if they want to.

Variations

Change the questions to suit your group. Make more of them silly, or more of them serious. Make them seasonal or custom design them for your audience.

Activity contributed by Cynthia Sosnowski, Stone Harbor, New Jersey.

Asset-Building Grand Pandemonium

Do everything listed here and get signatures to prove it!

Find a person who lives within 40 miles of you but whom you don't know. Have her or him sign here: ➡ _____

Find someone who knows how to play a musical instrument. Have her or him sign here: ➡ _____

Find someone who does volunteer work in the community. Have her or him tell you about it and sign here: ➡ _____

Ask two other people to join you in singing "Row, Row, Row Your Boat" in rounds, and have them sign here: ➡ _____

Find someone who has read a book in the past year just because he or she wanted to. Ask what it was, and have her or him sign here: ➡ _____

Find someone who is an active part of a faith community. Have her or him sign here: ➡ _____

Do your very best impersonation of a chicken for someone. Have her or him sign here: ➡ _____

Find someone who has a friend who is older or younger by at least 20 years than he or she is. Have her or him sign here: ➡ _____

Find someone who had a significant person in her or his past who provided the love and support he or she needed to get through a difficult time. Have her or him sign here: ➡ _____

If you finish filling in all other spaces before time is called, go back and find someone who signed your sheet and find out more about that person!

#5 ▶ Fill in the Blanks

Directions

Participants are seated around enough tables to accommodate the number of people. Ask participants to introduce themselves to others at their table by sharing their names and "filling in the blanks" in the two statements on the table tent.

Asset-Building Teaching Point

Close with this type of dialogue: "There are resources all around us! Giving children, teenagers, adults, and elders the opportunity to share their own unique gifts or talents can benefit everyone. Take a few minutes to answer the following questions: What gifts can you share with your community? What do you most want to receive from people in your community?"

Tips for Success

This activity works best when people are seated at tables of 6 to 10. Specify a time limit so that chatty participants will not over-shadow more introverted members of the group.

Variations

Tailor the questions to be more specific to what your presentation or meeting is about. For example, if you're working with a group of teachers, you might write, "What I'd most want to share with the students in my classroom is _____" or "What I'd most like to ask my students is _____."

You could also post the questions on an overhead projector for a large group, or put them on poster board and position it in the middle of a smaller group circle.

#6 ► The Circle Game

Directions

1. Tell participants that they're going to play a short game.

2. Instruct participants to form one large circle.

3. After the circle is formed, ask one participant to stand in the middle of the circle.

4. Distribute an index card and a piece of masking tape to each participant.

5. Instruct each person in the circle to tape the index card to the floor in front of her or him.

6. When all the participants have taped their cards to the floor give them the following instructions. The leader begins in the center and says something like:

- "When I say, 'Begin,' I'll ask the person standing in the center of the circle to describe a quality or aspect, for example, 'All my friends who [are afraid of heights, were born in Texas, wear glasses, are parents]…'"

- "If the descriptor fits you, you must immediately vacate your spot in the circle and try to move to another spot that has been vacated by someone else."

- "You may not move to a spot that is immediately next to you in the circle, even though it may have been vacated by your neighbor. The person inside the circle should also attempt to find a vacant place in the circle to stand."

- "Since there will always be one less spot marked by a card than there are participants, one person will always be left without a place in the circle. That person is the next to stand in the middle and call out 'All my friends who . . .'"

7. Confirm that participants understand the instructions and then begin.

8. Play the game for five to seven rounds.

Asset-Building Teaching Points

After the activity ask, "How does the game we just played remind you of programming for youth?" Allow a few minutes for participants to share their ideas. If they are not addressed, be sure to highlight various points; for example, programming often involves a lot of scrambling, it can be a lot of fun, sometimes we expend a lot of energy and aren't really sure of the outcome.

Tip for Success

It is important to have enough space available for this activity so that people have enough room to move around. This activity assumes easy and complete mobility for all of the participants. If this is not true for your group, you may want to use a different activity.

Adapted with permission from James Conway,
Integrating Assets into Congregations: A Curriculum for Trainers
(Minneapolis: Search Institute, 2000).

#7 ▶ Back to the Assets

Purpose: To help participants become more familiar with the assets and how they are nurtured in young people.

Suggested Group Size: 12 to 100.

Estimated Time: 10 minutes.

Materials Needed: Strips of paper with one asset printed on each one for each participant; masking tape; full list of 40 developmental assets from pages ix–x (one for each person).

Directions

1. Tape a strip of paper with an asset printed on it to the back of each participant without showing it to her or him first. Provide each person with a list of the assets for reference during the activity.

2. Ask participants to mingle, introducing themselves and asking each other this question to help them determine which asset is on their back: "What would you do to help a young person strengthen the asset I have on my back?"

3. As participants guess which assets are taped to their backs, they can move the strips to their name tags, folders, or other visible areas.

4. Have participants continue to circulate, asking and answering the question, until all have guessed the asset on their backs.

Asset-Building Teaching Points

Each asset addresses an important issue affecting our young people. When we take the time to think about how we can build assets, one at a time, we realize how easy it can be. Every day we can take small steps toward making the lives of our children and adolescents a little bit better.

Tips for Success

Have strips of paper and tape ready before the session begins. It's also a good idea to be certain that participants are familiar with the asset framework.

Variation

If you have a large group, pretape strips of paper and stick them on edges of plastic plates. Divide into small teams and give each team a plate, asking a team member to do the taping. Then ask to the team to circulate around the room and do the exercise with other teams. An alternative question for this activity might be, "What would it look like if this asset were well developed in a young person's life?"

Two-Circles Discussion

> **Purpose:** To help participants learn each other's names and begin a discussion of the developmental assets.
>
> **Suggested Group Size:** 10 to 40.
>
> **Estimated Time:** 10 minutes.
>
> **Materials Needed:** None.

Directions

1. Form two teams. Ask one team to form a circle, facing out. Have the other team surround them with a circle. Each person in the outer circle should face a person in the inner circle. For odd-numbered groups, work in a ratio of 2:1.

2. Ask participants to introduce themselves to the people they are facing and answer one of the questions listed below (the leader chooses the question). Then have participants in the outer circle move one space to the left and repeat the question (or the leader can ask a different question). Repeat as many times as desired.

3. Possible questions:

- Who was (or, for youth, is) your favorite neighbor when you were a child? Why?
- If you could start a club or organization for young people, what kind of organization would you start?
- When you were a youth, which adult did you most want to be like? Why?
- What do you think is one of the most important things that congregations, schools, and neighborhoods offer young people?
- Who expected (expects) the most of you when you were in school? Did (do) their expectations motivate you or frustrate you?
- What rule do you think is most important for families to have? Why?

- Where did (do) you do homework? Why?
- What do you love to learn about?
- Which culture besides your own are you most interested in? Why?
- What is something that gives your life a sense of meaning and purpose?
- What is one of your favorite ways to show other people that you care about them?
- Tell about something that happened recently in your neighborhood that showed people supporting or caring for each other.

Asset-Building Teaching Points

The framework of developmental assets was created to help us guide, support, love, and respect our youth. When we reflect on some of these aspects of our lives and what makes us tick, it allows us to see what we have in common with the youth around us and how we may be different. We can use this insight to find ways to engage with each other around our interests.

Tips for Success

Even if participants already know each other fairly well, this particular activity is likely a good way to spend your time. It is surprising how often people don't know these things about one another. This activity can serve as a more interesting, lively way to have introductions.

Variation

Before the meeting, inflate enough balloons for everyone to have one. Use a marker to write letters or numbers on pairs of balloons so that there are two balloons with each letter or number. Have participants stand in a large group and bat the balloons around. Play music if you like. At your signal, each person holds a balloon and finds the person with the matching letter or number to introduce her- or himself to and answer one of the questions. Repeat as many times as you wish.

#9 **What Shape Are You In?**

Directions

1. Give each person a pipe cleaner or a piece of clay.

2. Form into teams of 4 to 6.

3. Ask each person to make a sculpture to show her or his answer to the question, "What shape do you feel like as we begin this meeting?"

4. Have team members introduce themselves to each other, sharing their sculptures.

Asset-Building Teaching Points

Working for the good of our communities can be an exhausting and sometimes thankless effort. As asset builders we must remember to lift up not only our youth but also the people who champion the tremendous responsibility of making a difference in young people's lives. Efforts can fail, not because of a lack of need, but because of a lack of support. Coordinators and planners burn themselves out trying to take on too much. So today, let each one of us make a commitment to notice what shape we are in, ask for support when we need it, and be a shoulder to lean on when times get tough for others.

Tips for Success

Depending on the variety of issues or concerns surrounding your audience's asset-building efforts, responses to this activity can range from hopeful to skeptical. It's important to acknowledge the concerns of the group. Referring them to other resources or follow-up activities after the meeting may be a good way to help them get what they need without spending too much time on this activity.

Variation 1

Instead of using children's molding clay or pipe cleaners you can ask participants to draw what they feel like on a piece of paper with markers or you can ask them to describe "what shape they're in" by comparing themselves to an animal or automobile. For example, a turtle might want to pull her head in and not get involved. Or you can have a variety of shapes of photos available for participants to choose from and ask participants to select a symbol or photo that reflects "how they feel." You might start this conversation off by writing on a sheet of poster board, "In my asset-building efforts I feel like a _____ ."

Variation 2

If participants know each other well, you could use this as an opportunity for them to see how they perceive each other. Form a circle and ask one participant at a time to serve as the "clay" to be molded by the rest of the group. The group moves or "sculpts" the person in the middle in a manner that they feel represents the person's strengths and contributions. Once they are finished, ask the group to explain why they molded the person the way they did. Say something like, "Each of us has different and complementary contributions to make."

Variation contributed by Jim Williams, Junction City, Kansas.

Openers, Icebreakers, and Mixers

#10 ▶ Name Tag Sandwich

> **Purpose:** To get participants thinking about their role as asset builders.
>
> **Suggested Group Size:** Any size.
>
> **Estimated Time:** 5 minutes.
>
> **Materials Needed:** Plain name tags; pens, pencils, or markers.

Directions

1. Ask each participant to write her or his name on a name tag, leaving space at the top and bottom.

2. Ask participants to recall people who have had a positive impact on their lives in small ways and big ways. Tell participants to write the name of one such person in small letters above their name.

3. Then ask participants to identify a youth for which they personally are an asset builder. Ask them to write the name of the youth in small letters under their name.

4. Invite participants to tell someone nearby about the names on their name tag.

Asset-Building Teaching Points

Each one of us can be an important link in asset-building connections. The people who had a positive impact on our lives as youth can serve as perfect examples for how we can show the young people in our lives we care. Today let us reflect on these people of significance and remember how important they are to us and to the people whose lives we touch.

Tips for Success

It's very important to ask participants to recall people who positively influenced their lives in the past. Without this focus, people may recall negative experiences, which is not the purpose of the activity. Also, consider using oversized name tags to give people more room to write.

Variation

If participants know each other well, begin by asking them to write their own names, then encourage them to sign the bottom of the name tags of other participants who have been asset builders for them. Then ask participants to invite others to sign the top of their name tags. Highlight the idea that we often don't know the ways in which we touch the lives of others.

Activity contributed by Marilyn Peplau, New Richmond, Wisconsin.

#11 ▶ Birthday Roll Call Mixer

Purpose: To help participants learn one another's names, exchange some brief information, and start thinking about asset building.

Suggested Group Size: At least 8.

Estimated Time: 10 minutes.

Materials Needed: None.

Directions

1. Ask participants to line up in the order of their birthdays, designating one side of the room as January and one as December. If your group is very large, you many need to form more than one line.

2. Beginning with the first person in line, count off teams of 3 or 4. Have teams introduce themselves to each other, then discuss one question that pertains to your meeting, such as:

- What asset-building activity has been successful for your organization (or community)?
- What are you currently doing to build assets in young people?
- How are youth involved in your community initiative?

Asset-Building Teaching Points

As this activity tells us, finding something in common with someone you don't know isn't as hard as it sounds and can be a fairly easy way to start building a relationship. Really that's what building assets is all about—putting a little effort into building relationships between youth and adults, youth and other youth, and between adults who can provide support and encouragement to one another in their asset-building efforts.

Variation

Ask participants to form their lines without speaking and then check the accuracy of the sequence. It's generally quite amazing how creatively and accurately they determine the order.

#12 ▶ Block Exchange

Directions

1. Scatter the blocks around the room before participants arrive.

2. When your group is assembled, describe assets as the building blocks for healthy, caring, and responsible youth development. Then ask each participant to find one block.

3. Then ask participants to pair up and exchange names and blocks, describing how they build the assets on their blocks. Each will take the new block he or she has received and reintroduce her- or himself to another person, exchanging blocks again. Continue this until the group is mingling and talking.

Asset-Building Teaching Points

Ask participants, "How is this activity symbolic of asset building?"(Assets can never get used up, can be acquired, are cumulative, are additive.) Then ask participants to display the blocks in a central location of the meeting room. The arrangement of the blocks can be discussed and rearranged as the meeting or presentation progresses.

Tips for Success

This is a good activity for affirming the asset building people are doing but may not have recognized. Be sure to prepare the blocks (writing asset names) before your presentation. Also, make sure to have enough blocks for all participants. You may need more than one set for larger groups. If you have more blocks than people, double up on the number given to each person, or if the group will meet more than once, use them at a future meeting.

Variation

Instead of wooden blocks use foam blocks or small cardboard boxes.

Activity contributed by Marilyn Peplau,
New Richmond, Wisconsin.

Section 2

Build Strengths Together:
Team-Building Exercises and Games

#13 ▶ Group Juggling

Directions

1. Have participants stand in a circle. If your group is larger than 12, make an inner circle and an outer circle with half the participants in each. The inner circle will juggle first while the outer circle claps a rhythm and then the two circles will switch places.

2. Toss one ball to a person, saying that person's name before you pass the ball. That person then tosses it to another, saying that person's name first. The rule to emphasize here is that each person always tosses the ball to the same person so that the ball is passed around in the same pattern over and over. After three or four tosses have been made, start a second ball. Keep adding balls until all are in motion within the circle. When one of the balls drops and the pattern breaks, start over with one ball until the circles become fairly proficient.

Asset-Building Teaching Points

We depend on the cooperation of each other to keep the ball rolling—or in this case, flying—in our efforts. When we work together we can accomplish a number of tasks, more than we ever could alone.

Tip for Success

It's a good idea to do a round or two with one ball to give participants a chance to get used to the activity, then add balls in the next stage.

Variation

To make the activity a little more challenging, include a variety of objects that are safe to throw, such as balloons, rubber chickens, and Frisbees.

#14 ▶ Hula Hoop Game

Directions

1. Ask participants to form a circle or several circles around the room. Pick up a hula hoop, put your arm through it, and place it on your shoulder. Ask participants to hold hands.

2. Tell the group that the object of the game is to pass the hula hoop around the circle without dropping their hands. (In order to do this, each will need to pass the hoop over the head of the person next to her or him and let it drop down to that person's feet. The next person steps through it and it is pulled over their heads and so on.) *Note:* Do not give participants instructions on how to do this. Let them work it out for themselves first. If there are several groups, a little competition may make it more interesting.

3. After the group accomplishes the task, congratulate the group and encourage them to congratulate each other! Briefly discuss any problems or challenges and how to solve them. Then demonstrate the best way to do this task as described above. Ask the group to try it again.

4. After the second try, the presenter will put the hula hoop on her or his shoulder.

Asset-Building Teaching Points

Holding the hand of one participant, demonstrate what happens when the participant tries to pass the hula hoop to you and you don't cooperate. For example, move your hand the opposite way of the hoop. Discuss the implications of a lack of cooperation in schools, congregations, or communities (depending on your audience). Build on any positive points you saw during the exercise, such as someone encouraging a team member, and talk about the benefits of group problem solving.

Tip for Success

Depending on the group it may take some time for them to get the hang of this activity. Keep encouraging participants to successfully complete the task.

#15 ▶ Each One Teach One

> **Purpose:** To help participants explore how to explain assets to others.
>
> **Suggested Group Size:** 16 to 100.
>
> **Estimated Time:** 15 minutes.
>
> **Materials Needed:** Eight sheets of flip chart paper; at least 24 markers in various colors.

Directions

1. After your presentation on the basics of the developmental assets, divide participants into 8 teams.

2. Assign each team one of the asset categories. Ask them to think of a way to teach the large team how to build that asset category in communities. Give each team one or two pieces of flip chart paper (two pieces is best to avoid ink bleeding through onto tables) and at least three markers. Encourage teams to be as creative as they like with their paper and in their teaching.

3. Allow about five to ten minutes' prep time and then one minute per team presentation.

Asset-Building Teaching Point

Each one of us has the ability to teach someone else about the assets. Just think of how positive and effective it would be if each of us took time to share what we know about asset building with at least one other person in our community.

Tip for Success

Watch the clock on presentations! Have a sign that says "15 seconds remaining," then tell teams when their time is up.

Variation

Ask participants to name ways in which assets in their team's category are currently being built in their community. Affirm the good start they have in building assets.

Purpose: To provide a break during a presentation to allow participants to share a few ideas about asset building with each other.

Suggested Group Size: Any size.

Estimated Time: 3 minutes per break.

Materials Needed: Bell or other noisemaker.

Directions

1. Have participants form teams of 3. Tell them that each person will have 30 seconds of uninterrupted time to talk about one of the assets—specifically, how to help build it in young people.

2. Tell teams that the person who lives farthest from your present location is the first speaker.

3. Read one of the assets and its definition. Ring the bell for the first speaker to begin her or his 30-second presentation on how to build that asset.

4. After 30 seconds, ring the bell. Read another asset and its definition and ring the bell for the next person's opportunity to speak.

5. After 30 seconds, ring the bell. Read another asset and its definition and ring the bell for the last person in each team to speak.

6. Repeat process as desired.

Asset-Building Teaching Points

Asset building doesn't have to be a difficult task. We already have the ability within us to make a difference in the lives of young people. Taking 30 seconds to think about how to go about that may not seem like much, but it's the little efforts we make every day that can really make a difference to a young person.

Tip for Success

If the group is large, consider showing each asset name on an overhead projector to reduce the time needed to repeat the instructions.

Variation

Depending on the focus of your presentation, shape the question to fit your needs. For example, instead of focusing on how to build each asset you could ask participants why they believe the asset is important, how they have or have not experienced the asset, or to identify community resources for each asset.

#17 ▶ Crossing the Ragin' River

Purpose: To practice problem-solving skills and teamwork.

Suggested Group Size: At least 8 people in two teams of 4 each; can accommodate larger groups with additional materials and space.

Estimated Time: 20 to 25 minutes.

Materials Needed: Ten 2 x 2-foot carpet squares.

Directions

1. Place the pieces of carpet in a row approximately 18–24 inches apart. Ask four participants (the first team) to stand on the first four squares facing the middle of the room and then ask another four participants (the second team) to stand on the remaining squares facing the first team.

2. Give the group the following scenario: Two groups of people are hiking in the "Foggy Bottom Woods." Approaching from opposite sides, the groups come upon a raging river coincidentally called the "Ragin' River." Through the dense fog, the leaders of the two groups see a series of stepping-stones leading across the river. Although they can't see the opposite shore, each leader begins to lead her or his group across.

As they carefully step from one slippery stone to the next, both leaders eventually realize that another group of hikers is approaching them. Both groups meet right in the middle of the river. Each leader insists that the other group back up and allow her or his group to pass. The conversation becomes a heated argument and neither side is willing to back up because of how dangerous it would be to do so.

3. Give the groups the following instructions: "The rest of this story will be played out by all of you. Your challenge is to safely get both groups across the river without anyone going backward. You may advance forward to the next stone or help someone pass you in either direction, but no one is allowed to go back."

4. Allow the two groups 10 minutes to come up with their own ideas for a solution. If a solution can't be found, narrate the following instructions to the participants (for the sake of clarification give each group four identical titles such as Captain, Lieutenant, Sergeant, and Private):

a. Both Captains decide to take a step to the middle to discuss the problem and formulate a plan.

b. Finally the two Captains agree. The Right Group Captain begins by jumping (or climbing) over the Left Group Captain to say hello to the Left Group Lieutenant.

c. The Left Group Captain takes two steps forward to meet the Right Group Lieutenant.

d. The two Lieutenants jump over the Captains and meet in the middle to discuss the progress of both groups.

e. Not wanting to be left out, both groups' Sergeants take one step toward the middle to meet the opposite side's Captain and hear what is going on.

f. The Right Group Captain introduces her or himself to the Sergeant and then jumps to the left one space with the Lieutenant and the Sergeant following her or him.

g. The Left Group Captain takes one step forward, and her or his team members take one step to keep up.

h. The Right Group Captain takes one final step and turns to watch the progress; the Lieutenant and Sergeant take one step left.

i. The Left Group Captain takes one step right to meet with the Right Group Private. They say hello, and the Right Group private takes two large steps to keep up with the others in his group.

j. The Left Group Captain takes one final step forward, and the Lieutenant hurries over to join her or his leader by taking two steps forward. The Left Group Sergeant quickly follows.

k. The Left Group Private continues another two steps to catch up with the group.

l. The Right Group Private stops to talk with the Left Group Private until the Right Group Captain yells for her or him to continue. He or she takes one step, and both teams have completed the task.

Asset-Building Teaching Points

After the activity is completed, ask participants questions similar to the following:

- What did you learn about teamwork and cooperation from this activity?
- Did you consider the task easy, moderate, or difficult and why?
- How do you think this activity relates to our work in communities to build assets?
- What are some of the obstacles that you and your "team" have come up against?
- Were you able to find a solution?

Variations

If carpet squares are not available for this activity, pieces of cardboard (taped to the floor) or two-foot squares marked on the floor can also be used.

Activity contributed by Jim Williams, Junction City, Kansas.

#18 ▶ Community Puzzle

Directions

1. Based on the number of participants you expect, choose a puzzle that will provide about five pieces per person. If you have more than 25 participants, use more than one puzzle and have participants work in teams.

2. Assemble the puzzle ahead of time. Carefully take the puzzle apart in sections of five pieces. Put each section in a separate plastic sandwich bag.

3. Give participants each (except for one) a bag with a puzzle section and ask them to assemble their sections of the puzzle.

4. Next, tell them that they are to reconstruct the entire puzzle on the table top in five minutes or less. Tell them that the only person who may speak is the one who did not receive a bag of pieces. This person is the troubleshooter who will assist in assembling the puzzle. Give the troubleshooter the box cover with the picture of the completed puzzle. Play the music as they work.

Asset-Building Teaching Points

After the puzzle is reassembled, guide the discussion with these questions:

- What did you learn about teamwork?
- How did having a deadline affect your work?

- What role did the music play?
- How did having a troubleshooter affect your work?
- How important was it to have someone who had a sense of your final goal—a vision?
- How is community work like a jigsaw puzzle? (There are boundaries; the pieces are connected; each piece is unique; we all carry important pieces of the puzzle; the solution is fragile; the whole is more than the sum of the parts; the pieces need someone to move them; a person who sees the big picture can help; there are some natural groupings; and so on.)
- How is community work different from a jigsaw puzzle? (Puzzle pieces cannot change and adapt like people in a community can; the puzzle is limited to one solution and there are many directions communities can take; puzzle pieces are not interchangeable and there is a lot of give-and-take in communities; and so on.)
- What will you remember about this exercise tomorrow?

Tips for Success

If you have several teams of 25 working, print discussion questions on a handout and designate a discussion leader for each group. Choose one troubleshooter for each puzzle.

Variation

Give each team a puzzle, but don't tell anyone how big it is or what it should look like. Afterward, talk about the similarities and differences they see in their asset-building efforts (e.g., it's harder when you don't have a clear picture or goal).

Draw an Asset Builder

Directions

1. After presenting information on the eight categories of assets, ask participants to work with a partner to draw an asset builder.

2. Give each pair one or two pieces of flip chart paper (two pieces is best to avoid ink bleeding through onto tables) and some markers.

3. Offer these instructions: With your own artistic flair, create an image of an asset builder. Draw a person with things that an asset builder should have (such as a big smile for greeting people, a baseball cap to symbolize play, big ears for listening). Label the elements of your drawings.

4. Allow about 10 minutes to work, then post drawings for all to admire.

Asset-Building Teaching Points

Take a look at the different types of asset builders that have been created. Notice that not one of them looks exactly the same as another. That's what makes this work so special: anyone can be an asset builder and it takes all kinds!

Tip for Success

Be sure to have enough space to work.

Variations

Instead of using flip chart paper and markers, you might want to use a variety of materials including newspaper, magazines, bits of cloth, glue, crayons, and glitter to make collages.

Or, invite participants to draw an image of whatever best represents the characteristics of an asset builder (e.g., a building, a game board, an animal, a person).

#20 ▶ Mission to Mars

Purpose: To practice problem-solving skills and to use the exercise as a springboard for discussing group behavior and dynamics.

Suggested Group Size: At least 4.

Estimated Time: 10 to 12 minutes

Materials Needed: Sets of about 10 to 12 interlocking blocks (such as Legos®) that are identical in size and shape, but not necessarily the same color for each team of four or five participants; plastic bags.

Directions

1. Before the meeting or presentation, the presenter will use interlocking blocks to build an object that resembles a spaceship.

2. Place a set of identical block pieces in small plastic bags (one set per team).

3. Before you begin the activity, hide the first object that you have preassembled under a box or towel.

4. Divide the group into teams of four or five.

5. Give participants the following scenario or create your own:

"Secret agents of a distant country have stolen a vital part for a top-secret space launcher. If they learn how the part works, they will ruin our plan to be the first to land on the planet Mars. Your mission is to go into the secret lab of the enemy, study the part for one minute, and memorize what you see. We can sneak you in, but the Secret Police will search you as you leave—therefore, you cannot touch it or take it with you. You must memorize how it is put together and then recreate it from memory."

6. Uncover and allow each team to look at the "part" for 1 minute. Then cover it again.

7. Hand each team a second set of blocks and ask them to reassemble the "part" from memory. Instruct them that the shape must be the same though the color may not be.

Asset-Building Teaching Points

When we work together as a team, almost any mission is very possible. Let's talk about how each group accomplished this task. Did teams find that certain people emerged as leaders? Who had the best memory? Who was the quiet observer who noticed the details? Each of us has unique talents and ideas that we bring to the table in situations like this and in our communities. Let's remember to appreciate those gifts and use them!

Tips for Success

If after five minutes or so, no significant progress is made, you might let one person have a 15- to 30-second look at the part again. You also might give hints now and then if participants are having difficulty. Contributor Jim Williams says, "A middle school group of gifted kids did one of mine in a minute and a half because they each took one level of the object and memorized just that level. Then each person worked on their level from the bottom up. Great problem solving skills."

Activity contributed by Jim Williams
Junction City, Kansas.

#21 ► Radioactive Eggs

Directions

1. Divide the group into teams of 4 to 6.

2. Place each team's eggs in their egg carton with the dish (or paper plate) approximately one foot away.

3. Tell each team that the eggs are radioactive and need to be moved from the egg carton to a safe place (the dish) without being touched by anything but the tools. Ask teams to solve this problem together creatively with only the tools provided.

Note: There are eleven tools and twelve eggs; the teams will need to determine, on their own, that they will need to alter one or more of the tools to transfer all twelve eggs.

4. Give each team the following guidelines:

a. Touch the eggs only with the tools provided.

b. Once a tool touches an egg, you must finish using the tool and then discard it.

c. Each tool can only be used once for one egg.

d. Move only one egg at a time. Each person must participate in moving the eggs.

e. The carton and dish must not be moved. The carton and dish may be held steady.

f. If an egg touches the table, floor, skin, clothes, or any other object, the egg must be discarded.

g. Participants will earn one point for each egg moved safely.

h. Participants may earn bonus points for:
Moving one egg of each color—2 points
Moving a green egg and a pink egg—2 points
Moving all eggs successfully—5 points

Asset-Building Teaching Points

Sometimes we don't have all the "tools" we'd like to have to build assets, either personally or as a community. However, there are still creative ways to make it happen. We should never let challenges or obstacles prevent us from doing our best. Teamwork is an opportunity for us to work together and tear down any barriers and find new solutions!

Tip for Success

"Before I do the activity Radioactive Eggs, I like to spend time discussing problem solving and brainstorming to encourage creative thinking," says co-creator Nancy Leyerzapf.

Variations

Instead of eggs and egg cartons, you might want to use lightweight blocks or Styrofoam shapes and cardboard boxes.

Activity contributed by
Nancy Leyerzapf and Shirley Luce,
Junction City, Kansas.

Build Strengths Together

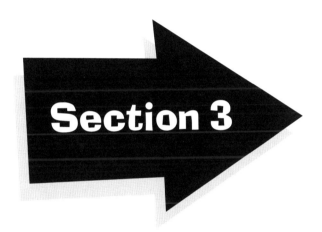

Section 3

Go Deeper with Assets:
Asset-Building Mind Benders
and Brain Teasers

#22 ▸ Mixed Messages

Directions

1. Ask a volunteer to leave the room.

2. While he or she is out, tell the rest of group that you are going to play the game "Hot and Cold." Instruct one-half of the group to guide the volunteer to the candy bar or other object you have chosen. Tell the other half of the group to guide the volunteer to a pen or book that is on the other side of the room. Tell groups that they will do this *at the same time.*

3. Call the volunteer in. Say that group will guide her or him to an object by saying, "hot" or "cold"; then let the game begin. After a minute or so, ask the volunteer, "How do you feel about this game? What do you think about your chances for succeeding?"

4. Ask the entire group, "What does this say about giving mixed messages to young people?" After a brief discussion, award the candy bar or other object to the volunteer for being a good sport.

5. Have participants get into teams of four and give each group several newspapers. Ask each person to find an example of something that sends a message that is very different from the messages asset initiatives are trying to give young people—something that contradicts asset building.

6. Ask small groups to share ideas about how to send consistent positive messages to youth in their communities. Let each table or group share an idea or two with the larger group.

7. Ask, "What will you remember about this exercise tomorrow?"

Asset-Building Teaching Point

Every day young people are bombarded with hundreds of mixed and confusing messages in homes, schools, among peers, on television programs, in music, and in movies. It's important for us to remain as clear and honest as we possibly can with youth and let them know that if they're feeling confused they can or should seek advice from an adult they trust.

Variation

Give each team flip chart paper and markers and ask them to compose the headlines for the front page of a newspaper that give positive and consistent messages about youth and about a community's feelings and expectations for them.

Adapted with permission from Bob Wittman, *Taking Asset Building Personally: A Guide for Planning and Facilitating Study Groups* (Minneapolis: Search Institute, 1999).

#23 ▶ Asset-Building Affirmations

Directions

1. Arrange participants so that people at the same table live in the same communities and neighborhoods or work for the same organizations.

2. Ask participants, "What type of relationships have you experienced in the past with young people?" Address issues such as the ease or difficulty of talking to a young person, or maintaining a relationship.

3. Distribute three cards to each participant. Also distribute the "Asset-Building Affirmations" handout, asking participants to read the material carefully.

4. Next, ask participants to choose two or three that they would like to accomplish (or invite them to add their own). Then write one of these affirmations down on each card. Ask participants to share what they've written with the people at their table. This will serve as a public declaration of their intentions.

Asset-Building Teaching Points

Close the activity with dialogue similar to the following: "Every morning for at least the next week, read and think about the affirmations you've chosen. Do this in a quiet place—for example, in your car in the parking lot. Display the affirmations in places that will remind you to act upon them, such as on your refrigerator or next to your phone."

Tip for Success

Don't worry about arranging the group by organization or community if the group is totally mixed.

Variations

If groups of people do work for the same organizations or live in the same communities, challenge them to pair off and become asset-building buddies or partners. Every so often—perhaps once a month–those partners can contact each other in some way and find out about one another's progress and offer support and encouragement to one another.

Asset-Building Affirmations

1. I'm a powerful asset builder in the lives of youth in my community.

2. I know and use young people's names regularly when I see them.

3. I focus daily on young people's gifts and talents.

4. I help youth use their strengths to overcome their deficits.

5. I regularly encourage other adults in my community to build assets with young people.

6. When young people are in trouble, I begin my interactions by focusing on their strengths.

7. Each day, I'm involved in spontaneous acts of asset building.

8. I'm expanding my positive influence by pursuing relationships with young people I don't know.

9. At least once a week, I do something for youth that goes beyond their normal expectations.

10. I work hard to maintain relationships with youth with whom I'm already connected.

11. I have high expectations for myself, my fellow community members, and young people in my community.

12. I take the time to listen when young people speak to me.

13. I take initiative in engaging young people positively.

14. I smile at and make eye contact with young people as I go about my day.

15. I believe that my power as an asset builder comes from the relationships that I develop with youth.

16. I engage young people positively at school and in the community.

#24 ▸ The Asset Difference Continuum

Purpose: To help participants further reflect on the difference asset building can make in a community.

Suggested Group Size: 6 to 40.

Estimated Time: 10 minutes.

Materials Needed: "The Asset-Building Difference" overhead transparency (from master); overhead projector; screen or blank wall.

Directions

1. Clear a long area in the room.

2. Display the overhead transparency, using a sheet of paper to reveal only one line at a time.

3. Designate different sides of the room as the two ends of the continuum represented in the shift described on the overhead and ask participants to position themselves to show where they feel their community is in the change process on each particular shift.

4. Invite participants to call out suggestions for how to help groups and individuals move from one side of the continuum to the other.

5. Repeat this for each item on the overhead or for a few items that are of most interest to the group.

Asset-Building Teaching Points

Every community goes through different stages of development in the process of becoming an asset-building place. Is your community taking the right steps toward becoming an asset-rich environment? Where do you see the most progress? What gets in the way? How can you ensure that you keep making progress?

Tips for Success

If you have a very large group and enough space you may want to have several lines doing the activity simultaneously. Also, if you have a diverse group of participants (race, ethnicity, age, gender), take time to reflect on differences in perceptions. For additional information see *All Kids Are Our Kids: What Communities Must Do to Raise Caring and Responsible Children and Adolescents,* by Peter L. Benson.

Variation

If the group is all from the same initiative, use this as an opportunity to compare "then and now." Select two or three continua and ask people to arrange themselves based on where the community was at the beginning of the initiative and then based on where and whether the community has changed. Where have they seen progress? What's most important for the community to work on? Why and how?

The Asset-Building Difference

FROM:

Problem focus

Youth as problems

Reactive behavior

Blaming

Professionals

Crisis management

Competition

Despair

TO:

Positive focus

Youth as resources

Proactive behavior

Claiming responsibility

Everyone

Vision building

Cooperation

Hope

#25 ▶ from Troubles to Treasures

> **Purpose:** To help participants assist each other in meeting the challenges faced by their initiatives. This is a great activity to intersperse throughout a meeting.
>
> **Suggested Group Size:** 6 to 60.
>
> **Estimated Time:** 5 minutes to set up; 3 minutes per activity.
>
> **Materials Needed:** One blank sheet of paper for each person; a large empty basket or box; tape; pens or pencils.

Directions

1. Near the beginning of your meeting or workshop, ask each person to take a moment to think about one challenge he or she is facing in her or his initiative or other asset-building commitment and to briefly write about it at the top of a blank sheet of paper.

2. Invite participants to wad their "troubles" (sheets) into a ball and toss them into the basket or box.

3. At some point during your meeting, ask participants to get into teams of three.

4. Toss each team one paper ball from the basket. Tell them to flatten the paper, read about the challenge, and then spend three to five minutes brainstorming possible ways to meet the challenge. They should write their brainstorming ideas directly on the sheet.

5. Tape up completed sheets in a central place where people can look at them during breaks or afterward.

6. Repeat this activity at two other times during the meeting so that all sheets from the basket are discussed.

7. At the end of the meeting, invite individuals to take their own sheets with them.

Asset-Building Teaching Points

Remember the old saying "Two heads are better than one"? In some situations, no matter how hard we try to come up with the right answers or information on our own, we end up at a dead end. Sometimes the best way to approach a challenge is to simply ask someone else for advice. He or she may have a whole new perspective that we can learn from.

Tips for Success

Explain the full activity to participants in advance so that they will write a challenge they are comfortable having others discuss. Encourage the group to select challenges that are "real" to them and not just a generic problem faced by initiatives.

Variations

"Solution Roundtable"—Form teams of 4 to 8 people. Ask each team to identify one issue or challenge they would like input on from others in the room. It's important to describe challenges in detail so that others have a clear understanding of issues involved. The team then passes their sheet to another team (establish a rotation). The second team spends around five minutes brainstorming potential solutions. Repeat rotation until all teams have seen sheets or until desired time has passed. The original team reviews potential solutions and identifies what they would like to implement.

#26 ▶ Changing Your Attitude

> **Purpose:** To help participants identify attitudes that help—as well as hinder—asset building.
>
> **Suggested Group Size:** 10 to 100.
>
> **Estimated Time:** 10 to 15 minutes.
>
> **Materials Needed:** As many sets of Attitude Cards (see directions) as needed for all participants to receive one card.

Directions

1. Before presenting this activity, create sets of Attitude Cards with either index cards or paper cut in 3 x 5-inch pieces. Each statement requires its own 3 x 5 card. Be sure to prepare enough so that every participant will receive at least one card and so that the companion card will also be distributed, allowing participants to pair off later in the activity.

2. Use the following list of contrasting statements:

a. I need to focus on young people's problems.

I need to focus on young people's strengths.

b. Only professionals can build assets in young people.

Everyone can build assets in young people.

c. Young people absorb resources.

Young people are resources.

d. Building developmental assets is a program.

Building developmental assets is a way to interact with young people.

e. I should try to affect primarily those young people who seem to be troubled or who are troubling me.

I should try to affect all the young people I come into contact with every day.

f. How other adults behave around young people doesn't really concern me.

I hold other adults accountable for their actions toward young people.

g. We're already building assets.

We need to build assets more intentionally.

3. Distribute one Attitude Card to each participant (large groups will have multiples). Ask each participant to think about the idea expressed on her or his card. Does it help or hinder asset building? Next, ask participants to find a person with the companion card that gives the statement opposite to that of their own. For example, if a card reads "Young people absorb resources," the companion card would read "Young people are resources."

4. Participants will have 10 minutes to find their "companion" and discuss which one of the two statements builds assets and which describes their own attitudes.

Asset-Building Teaching Points

Many of us may have come here today looking for ways to transform our communities. For this to happen, we need to first find ways to transform ourselves. Building assets in communities often requires a shift in the way we think and act—it's a different way of looking at things. The attitudes we addressed in this activity reflect the attitudes of many in our communities. What we would hope to do today is to come away with ideas to change less-than-positive attitudes to asset-building attitudes.

Tip for Success

Be sure to give yourself adequate time to prepare the materials needed before beginning this activity.

Variation

A number of materials such as colored cardboard, stickers, markers, and glue can be used to create the Attitude Cards in this activity. Feel free to be as creative as you want.

Directions

1. Before your meeting or presentation, inflate the balloons and label them with a permanent or dry erase marker as indicated:

- Inflate one balloon completely. Label it "31–40 Assets."

- Inflate three balloons three-fourths full. Label each of them "21–30 Assets."

- Inflate four balloons one-half full. Label each of them "11–20 Assets."

- Inflate two balloons one-fourth full. Label each of them "0–10 Assets."

2. Have participants stand close together in a circle. (Six to 16 persons is best, but this can work with up to 20. If you have a large group, have smaller teams create webs simultaneously.)

3. Give the roll of streamer to one person. Have that person tell one role that he or she currently has as an asset builder (such as neighbor, parent, mentor, coach, aunt, friend, or grandparent). The person holds the end of the streamer and tosses the roll to a person who is at least two people away. That person then tells her or his role as an asset builder, hangs on to the streamer, and tosses the roll to another person. Continue until all have

participated. If the group is small, go around again until all of the streamer is in the web.

4. Comment on all the acts of individual asset building that work together to make a strong community web. Encourage the group to pull on the streamers to "tighten up" their web so that it is the best one possible for supporting their youth.

5. Tell the group that their community has 10 young people. Toss the largest balloon on the web and challenge them to keep it supported. Point out that for every 10 young people, we know that about one experiences 31-40 assets. Toss the 21-30 balloons on the web, pointing out that about 30 percent of our young people have this level of assets. Next toss the 11-20 balloons, challenging the group to keep them in the web and telling them that 43 percent experience this level of assets. Finish with the two smallest balloons representing 0-10 assets for 20 percent of youth. (Inevitably, some balloons will be on the floor by now.)

6. Now, tell the group that anyone born in January, February, or March has done their fair share for young people. They can now stop building assets and drop their part of the web.

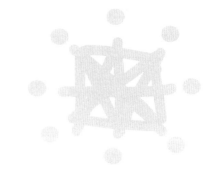

Asset-Building Teaching Points

Lead a discussion with questions like these:

- What does this show about the power of individuals?

- What happened when some people decided they had done enough (stopped participating in asset building)?

- What does this show about the power of communities?

- What would it take to create a strong web of support for all our youth?

- What will you remember from this exercise tomorrow?

Tip for Success

As the web is being built, encourage people to keep their examples brief. If participants start sharing stories, it will make the activity too long.

Variations

If your meeting space allows, lay the web on the floor with the balloons as a visual reminder for the rest of your time together. You can also use various size balloons (5, 7, 9, or 12 inch).

Adapted with permission from Bob Wittman, *Taking Asset Building Personally: A Guide for Planning and Facilitating Study Groups* (Minneapolis: Search Institute, 1999).

#28 The Search Game

Purpose: To help participants reflect on creative community planning processes.

Suggested Group Size: 6 to16.

Estimated Time: 25 to 30 minutes.

Materials Needed: Eight index cards.

Directions

1. On each card, write one of these words: "There are many ways to reach your goal."

2. Ask three volunteers to leave the room.

3. Hide the eight cards around your meeting space so that they are out of sight. Make sure that the participants in the room know the location of each card. Instruct them that they may not speak to the volunteers, except to answer yes or no to questions.

4. Invite the three volunteers back into the room. Give them these instructions:

a. Find the eight cards that are hidden in this room.

b. You may ask only questions that can be answered by yes or no.

c. You must ask everyone in the room one question before you can ask a person a second question. Other than that, there is no limit to the number of questions you can ask.

d. After you find the eight cards, use them to make a statement.

e. Let the game proceed without additional comment, except to remind participants that they may not speak other than to answer questions. Make sure that each person is asked a question once before the second round of questions begins.

Asset-Building Teaching Points

After the cards are found and the statement put together, discuss these questions:

- What did the searchers do?
- What did the searchers learn?
- What did the other participants learn?
- Do you agree or disagree with the statement that was formed? Why?
- How is this exercise an illustration of planning for community action? How is it not?
- What will you remember about this exercise tomorrow?

Tips for Success

Do not try this activity if you have less than 30 minutes. It often takes 20 minutes to find the cards and it is important not to "bail out" the searchers or to shortchange the discussion. You may wish to use some visual indication of who has been asked a question in this round (e.g., once you've been asked a question, cross your arms).

Variations

Instead of using index cards you could make your own puzzle pieces with a thick piece of paper or cardboard. Write a word of the statement on each puzzle piece and instruct the group in the same way. Or you could come up with a different statement more relevant to your group.

#29 Asset Kid Puzzle

Purpose: To engage participants in a conversation about assets.

Suggested Group Size: At least 12.

Estimated Time: 12 to 15 minutes.

Materials Needed: Sheet of poster board or other lightweight cardboard at least three feet long; markers; scissors.

Directions

1. Draw the outline of a young person in an active pose on the poster board. Color in some hair, then divide the rest of the outline into 40 puzzle pieces, each labeled with the name and number of the assets.

2. If your community has survey data, color in the assets that ranked highest, coloring the number of pieces that equals the average number of assets in your community. For example, if the average number of assets in your community is 17, color in the puzzle pieces that name the 17 highest-rated assets in your youth.

3. If you do not have survey data, color in the average number of assets experienced by youth from an aggregate sample, Asset #'s 1, 9, 10, 12, 13, 15, 18, 19, 20, 21, 22, 24, 28, 29, 30, 38, 39, 40. (The average number of assets in communities surveyed by Search Institute is 18.)

4. Cut the pieces apart. Then reassemble the puzzle for the group.

5. You may use the puzzle as a whole to help illustrate the point that while one can construct a puzzle with a few pieces, more pieces make it a stronger picture. Ask small groups to discuss one of the assets that is not colored and to think of ways your community can strengthen it.

Asset-Building Teaching Points

To date, Search Institute has analyzed data from nearly 100,000 young people in 23 states across the county who have taken the survey that measures the 40 assets. From that research, we have learned that the average youth in our study experiences 18 of the assets. What does that mean for our community? It means that there is still a lot to be done to make young people feel valued and valuable. This activity reminds us that youth can't just have some of the things they need to be whole and happy, they need all of the pieces to fit together.

Variation

Give pairs or small teams one piece of the puzzle and have them discuss the asset named on it and how it can be strengthened. Then construct the puzzle as a group, pointing out how the average number of assets in your community is not enough to support whole and healthy young people. Ask small groups to each discuss one of the assets that is not colored and to think of ways your community can strengthen them.

Adapted with permission from an idea submitted by Joan Meis Wilson to *Assets: The Magazine of Ideas for Healthy Communities & Healthy Youth* (Minneapolis: Search Institute, Summer 1998).

#30 Redesigning Your Community

Directions

1. Before the activity begins, label each flip chart sheet with titles similar to the following:

- In schools
- In congregations
- Among businesses
- For parents/families
- For adults/mentors
- For law enforcement officials
- For any organization
- For government agencies
- For child-care providers
- For the media
- In neighborhoods

2. Place the sheets and markers around the room. Ask each participant to think of specific ways to make her or his community more conducive to building assets. Ask participants to pretend that they have the power to redesign their communities. Each easel sheet represents one of the 10 areas they may address.

3. Give participants the following instructions:

a. Choose the three areas that most interest you.

b. Take a few minutes to think about what specifically you would like to do in these areas. Think creatively; don't be limited by traditional ways of doing things. What can you do physically, emotionally, and socially to build assets in your community?

c. After a few minutes you will be asked to write your ideas down on the appropriate sheet. When several people have gathered by a sheet, choose one person to record ideas. You will be told when to move on to another sheet.

4. Begin. Give participants about five minutes per station or area to discuss and record.

5. Reconvene the group and choose several volunteers to share their ideas.

Asset-Building Teaching Points

Each part of our community can become a place to build assets. It just takes our creativity and willingness to spread these very important messages to people like teachers, business owners, neighborhood organizations, media representatives, and law enforcement officials. The purpose of this activity was for us to brainstorm how we can go about making asset building and the best interests of youth our top priority every day.

Tips for Success

This activity can create a lot of conversation, so be careful to watch the time.

Variation

Personalize this activity by creating sheets that speak specifically to your audience. For example, if you are doing a presentation for teachers, you may target areas within school environments such as, "In the Classroom," "On the School Bus," and "In the Hallways."

Purpose: To remind participants of the importance of a supportive, encouraging environment for youth.

Suggested Group Size: Any.

Estimated Time: 10 minutes.

Materials Needed: The IALAC worksheet from page 45 (one for each participant).

Directions

1. Tell participants that IALAC stands for "I Am Lovable and Capable," and distribute the worksheets.

2. Give the group a story or scenario similar to the following:

Every young person should have the opportunity to feel loved and capable. Unfortunately, some parents, teachers, and other adults in our communities don't always make supporting and encouraging our youth a priority. Listen to a story about a typical day for a young man named John. Each time you hear something in the story that could lead John to believe that maybe he is not so capable and lovable, tear off a piece of your IALAC sign.

John is 12 years old. He lives in the country and attends middle school in a nearby town. John awakens to the sound of his mother pounding on his bedroom door, yelling, "John, you better get up. I've called you three times already and you're going to miss the school bus if you don't get your lazy bones out of bed." John doesn't remember hearing his mother call him, but he rolls out of bed. He sees that it is late and he doesn't have time to take a shower or eat any breakfast.

As John races out the door, his father yells at him, "You better get home right after school tonight. You have chores to do and I'm not doing them for you." John had wanted to stay after school tonight to try out for the school play. He realizes that that isn't an option.

As John gets on the school bus, the bus driver tells John he has to sit in the front seat. One of the little kids on the bus said John had pushed him yesterday. He didn't do it, but there was no sense in arguing. The bus driver never believes him anyway.

John takes out his math book to study for his test that day. When he gets to school, he forgets his book on the bus and has to run back to get it. The principal meets him at the school door and says, "Almost late again, John. I suppose I'll be seeing you in my office later, if this is any sign of how your day is going to go."

At lunch, John's friends dare him to ask Jenny to the school dance being held on Friday night. John really likes Jenny, but he is nervous about asking her. When he finally gets up the nerve to ask her, she says, "Whatever made you think I would go to the dance with you? No way!" His friends watch and laugh.

John really messes up on his math test. One wrong formula makes him get half of the problems wrong. The math teacher gives him an angry look as he corrects his paper, but John doesn't have enough time to explain.

After school, the math teacher catches John in the hall and wants to talk to him about his math test. John misses his bus and has to walk four miles home. His father is angry and makes him work through supper to finish his chores. After he finishes, John eats supper alone. John stays up late to finish his homework. He will probably be tired in school tomorrow.

Asset-Building Teaching Points

Following this story, ask participants how John's day could have been made better. How could the adults in his life help build assets? How could his peers help him? How could John work on building assets for himself?

Tips for Success

Before you tell the "story," demonstrate tearing of a piece off the IALAC sign so that participants don't get hung up on how big a tear should be. Also let participants know that it's okay to giggle or react if they can relate to having a day like this.

Variations

Change the story to fit the needs or interests of your audience; for example, "John" can become "Jennifer," the school setting can become a neighborhood setting, the rural town can became an urban environment. If time allows, invite participants to write a story about how John's day might have gone if the people in his life paid attention to asset building.

Activity contributed by Merry Klemme, Kewaunee, Wisconsin; a variation of the activity used with permission from Sidney Simon, *I Am Loveable and Capable: A Modern Allegory of the Classical Put-Down* (Niles, IL: Argus Communications, 1974).

IALAC

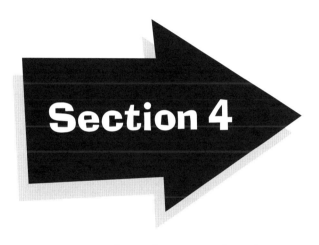

Section 4

Games for Youth and Adults: Intergenerational Activities

#32 ▸ Assets Draw

Directions

1. Create Asset Draw cards by writing an asset and a suggestion for a related picture to draw on a note card. (Or, create the cards on a computer and print on card stock.) Select assets and pictures to draw that will fit the age of your expected participants. For example:

■ **Asset #25**
Reading for pleasure: Young person reads for pleasure three or more hours per week.
Draw: A library card.

■ **Asset #1**
Family support: Family life provides high levels of love and support.
Draw: A hug and a smile.

■ **Asset #17**
Creative activities: Young person spends three or more hours per week in lessons or practice in music, theater, or other arts.
Draw: A musical note.

2. Explain that the young person should draw the suggested picture or another one that relates to the asset.

3. Ask the adult family member to try to guess the picture as it is being drawn. The game leader can read the asset to the adult as a clue if needed.

4. Award a small prize to the young person. Give the adult some information about asset building (available from Search Institute).

Asset-Building Teaching Points

Was it easy or difficult for you to think of something to draw? Is this asset something that your family already builds, or is it something you could work on strengthening? In what ways does your family build this asset? (Note: If participants are unfamiliar with the assets, this could also be a time to introduce the framework.)

Tip for Success

If you are using this in a carnival or fair booth, have one game leader per whiteboard or chalkboard.

Variation

You can also play a team version of this game, in a manner similar to Pictionary™.

 **Share the Wealth: Ideas of Value**

#33

Purpose: To collect and exchange ideas for asset building.

Suggested Group Size: At least 20.

Estimated Time: 5 minutes to set up, 5 minutes for each "exchange."

Materials Needed: Play money that is blank on one side (one piece for each person).

Directions

1. Give each person a piece of play money and ask her or him to write on the back of the bill her or his best asset-building idea (e.g., for introducing assets to adults, for building assets in congregations, for teaching youth about assets, or whatever topic you choose).

2. Pause several times during the meeting or workshop and announce that it's time to circulate the "money." Allow a few minutes for people to exchange play money, read what others have written, and jot down ideas of interest to them.

Asset-Building Teaching Points

Everyone has a valuable idea about asset building that they can share with others! We have to remember in this work that others can benefit from our experiences and we can learn from others. Why reinvent the wheel when we don't have to? When we share our wealth of ideas we all leave richer.

Tips for Success

If you can't find play money, make some on a computer, using clip art of currency on one side and leaving the back blank. Print on green paper and cut apart. If your time is very limited or your group is large, you could collect all the bills, compile the ideas into a single document, and send a copy to each participant after the meeting.

Variation

Print "checks" in the amount of "one asset-building idea"; have participants date and sign the "check" and write details of their idea on the back. Then ask participants to pair off to share ideas, make their check out to their partner, and exchange checks. If participants wish to use the idea they receive they can contact the originator (include phone numbers or email addresses).

#34 ► Bag of Rocks

Purpose: To illustrate the need for support and encouragement of youth in communities.

Suggested Group Size: 10 to 50.

Estimated Time: 10 to 12 minutes.

Materials Needed: One large and sturdy bag strong enough to carry 15 to 20 pounds (a backpack may be more suitable for youth, a briefcase or canvas bag might be better for adults); 10 to 12 smooth rocks the size of a large potato painted a solid color. (The rocks should be large enough for them to be written on and the words large enough to be seen by a group of people); the 40 developmental assets list from pages ix–x (one copy for each participant).

Directions

1. Before the presentation or meeting, write or paint words on each rock that express the different types of challenges youth can face in communities, such as violence, poverty, abuse, depression, suicide, smoking, alcohol use, illicit drugs, and sex. Then place the rocks in the bag.

2. Ask a volunteer to try to put the backpack on or to carry the canvas bag. Discuss with participants how heavy the bag is and how tired a person would be if he or she had to carry such a heavy load around all day long, day after day. Ask another volunteer to look in the bag and see what is making the bag so heavy.

3. Then ask the second volunteer to remove the rocks, one at a time, and read what is written on each to the rest of the group. Ask participants to discuss these challenges using the assets to help them determine solutions or ways in which others in the community

can help a young person overcome these issues. Encourage the group to use a statement similar to "The asset(s) that would help this load is (are)_____." As the rocks are being removed, ask the person carrying the bag if it feels easier to handle.

4. Continue the activity until the bag is empty. After the bag is empty, discuss how this exercise illustrates the fact that communities rally around youth and support them, the "burdens" that make young people's lives a challenge are easier to overcome.

Asset-Building Teaching Points

Carrying a heavy emotional burden all by ourselves isn't easy or healthy. When we don't have trusted family members or friends to help us, we struggle through even the simplest of tasks. Let's remember that the people we care about, especially our youth, need someone who will listen to them, support them, and encourage them.

Variation

A similar activity can be done focusing on positive influences. It may even serve as a second part to the first exercise. Gather 10 or 12 sponges or craft foam the size of small bricks. Write words or concepts that empower people such as family support, safety, high expectations, integrity, self-esteem, youth programs, caring neighborhood, and creative activities. Follow the directions for the first activity. This time talk about how easy the bag is to handle and how a bag full of these items can help us avoid carrying a bag full of rocks.

Activity contributed by Jim Williams,
Junction City, Kansas.

Intergenerational Activities

51

Purpose: To help participants learn one another's names and to think a bit about the assets that were (or are) present in their youth. This activity works great as something for people to do as they arrive before the starting time of a meeting or workshop.

Suggested Group Size: At least 8.

Estimated Time: 15 minutes.

Materials Needed: One activity sheet from page 53 for each person; pens.

Directions

1. Before beginning this activity, pick a chronological age at least three years younger than the youngest participant present.

2. Give each participant an activity sheet and a pen.

3. Ask participants to think of when they were a certain age (depending on what you decide) and to fill in the information about themselves in the first column.

4. Ask participants to mingle and talk to each other. As two people introduce themselves, suggest that they compare notes about their youth and determine if their experiences were similar or different. Once two people have talked about their experiences, they should sign each other's sheets in an appropriate box and then move on to meet and talk with others.

5. After participants have filled in at least eight of the ten boxes, have them sign sheets and put them in a container for a door prize. Or you could offer a small prize to everyone who collects eight signatures.

Asset-Building Teaching Points

When we think about our youth (or when we were younger), it's fun to think about the things that make or made us smile, the friends that we have and the types of activities we participated in. What's important to note, though, is that while many of us had some similar experiences, we also had some very different ones. The same is true of youth today. It can be easy to make generalizations or assume that we know what all youth need and want. But really, we can't know until we talk to them and get to know them as individuals.

Tip for Success

Keep an eye on the clock! This activity fosters lots of conversation.

Variation

To gain a perspective of different age groups, ask some participants to think about when they were eight, some 12, some 16. Then talk about how community experiences are different at different ages.

"When I was _____" Activity Sheet

About me . . .	Someone who had a similar experience . . .	Someone who had a different experience . . .
State that I lived in:		
I had this many siblings:		
My favorite thing to do with my time was:		
There were about ____ students in my grade at school.		
One way that adults outside my family showed their care and support for me was:		

#36 ▸ Asset Animals

Purpose: To help participants think about asset building in an imaginative way. This is a great activity to follow a break.

Suggested Group Size: At least 6.

Estimated Time: 5 to 7 minutes.

Materials Needed: None.

Directions

1. Ask participants to form groups of three.

2. Tell participants to introduce themselves to each other and to each complete this statement:

"To build an asset-rich relationship with a young person, I think it is most helpful to act like a (name of a nonhuman animal) because _____."

3. Depending on your agenda, you may not want to debrief immediately after this exercise and save the responses for use in a discussion of the characteristics of asset-building leaders.

Asset-Building Teaching Points

What types of animals did people mention today? What are some of reasons why these animals would make good asset builders? Animals can teach us a lot about working with others to accomplish our goals. For example, geese fly in formation and cheer each other on when they make the long flight south before winter hits. Wolves work together to hunt large game. How do others help and support you in your asset-building efforts?

Tip for Success

If you decide to use the variation, this activity can get pretty noisy. Be sure your environment is "noise-friendly."

Variation

Have groups of three decide on one animal, then present it to another group of three who will guess what they are. These groups of six can then discuss why they chose the animals they did.

#37 ▶ Protecting Our Future

Purpose: To help adult participants visualize the importance of youth throughout their meeting.

Suggested Group Size: At least 18.

Estimated Time: 15 minutes.

Materials Needed: About 25 sheets of 8 1/2 x 11-inch paper per group; markers.

Directions

1. Ask participants to name things in our society today that put young people in high-risk situations. Write each one on a separate sheet of paper. Continue until you have named 8 to 10 high-risk factors. Then give each sheet to a different person.

2. Ask for a volunteer to represent a 6th grader. Have this person stand in the front of the room.

3. Have the people with the high-risk factor sheets wad them into balls and throw them at the volunteer, trying to hit her or him. Comment on how the 6th grader needs some reinforcements to ward off all these negative influences. Collect the paper balls and return them to group members.

4. Now, ask the group to name all those who influence the life of a young person in positive ways (parents, teacher, religious leaders, peers, neighbors, and so on). Write each one on a sheet of paper, then ask several people to come to the front and hold the sheets. After you have about 10 people, arrange them in a large, loose circle around the 6th grader.

5. Ask the group to suggest ways to improve the support for the 6th grader. (Examples include telling positive influences to stand closer together and closer to the child, connecting positive influences with the child and with each other.) Move the circle of influences as directed by the group.

6. Now, have the persons holding the risk factors throw them at the 6th grader again. As a group, discuss what was different when the 6th grader was surrounded by support. Discuss who else might provide protection to the young person beyond those named in the activity. Then ask participants what they will remember about this activity tomorrow.

Asset-Building Teaching Points

Whether we like to admit it or not, as long as negative influences like underage drinking, tobacco use, and drug experimentation still exist, our young people are still very much at high risk. Open dialogue about how we can combat these behaviors is a good first step at solving the problem. The next step is turning words into actions.

Tip for Success

If you are using this as a demonstration in front of a very large group, make sure that the "actors" can be seen and heard by all. A sound system can be helpful.

Variation

If you have a large group, recruit additional leaders and ask each group of 18–20 to complete the exercise.

#38 ▸ Reframing

Directions

1. If the conversation during a meeting or presentation turns negative, place your face in the picture frame and ask, "Could you reframe that positively?"

2. Then hand the picture frame over to participants and invite them to share their opinions. The catch is that they have to do it in a positive way.

Asset-Building Teaching Points

An empty picture frame can serve as a humorous reminder that asset building means changing our attitudes and actions. This work is not always easy! But when we remember that the only way to accomplish our goals is to work together, we realize that a positive attitude is much more productive than a negative one.

Tip for Success

Remember to keep an encouraging attitude with participants. It will help set a positive mood for the presentation.

Activity contributed by Marilyn Peplau, New Richmond, Wisconsin.

#39 ▶ Asset Stretch

Purpose: To help groups visualize their thoughts about the importance of the assets and the progress of their work in building them.

Suggested Group Size: Any size.

Estimated Time: 5 to 10 minutes.

Materials Needed: None.

Directions

1. After presenting information on the eight categories of assets, ask all who are able to stand.

2. Invite them to use their arms (and the rest of their bodies!) to show how important they think each of the categories is for their community or organization. Read the categories, pausing after each one for participants to use their body language to tell how important they think it is. (For example, a person who thinks that the support assets are most important may stand on tiptoes and stretch both hands overhead. A person who feels they are less important may kneel down.)

3. Next, invite participants to use body language to show how well they think their community or organization is actually building each category of assets. Read the categories, pausing after each one for participants to use their body language to tell how well they feel those assets are being built. As you have time, invite participants' reaction to the exercise. Any surprises? Any questions?

Asset-Building Teaching Points

Sometimes it's a good idea to "stretch" yourself and think about where your community is in its asset-building efforts. Just as the responses here today have varied, different members of the community may have different ideas of what you can do to make the well-being of youth a priority. While most of us agree that all the categories are important, they are less likely to feel that they are doing really well in all categories. Take the time to listen to those voices; it could make a huge difference.

Tip for Success

If you're short on time, you might want to choose the categories you want to emphasize most in your presentation.

Variation

Select the asset category of particular interest to the group and use the assets in that category for the "asset stretch."

#40 ▶ Cars

Directions

1. Ask participants to form two even lines facing you. Each person in the front row should have another participant standing directly behind her or him. If the group is too large or if you end up with an odd number, ask these participants to leave the line. They may participate later.

2. Ask participants in the back row to place their hands on the shoulders of the person in front of them. Next ask the person in front to place their elbows at their sides and their hands out in front to them to serve as a "bumper." If there are extra participants, ask them to be the "obstacles." For example, two can hold their hands above their heads to form a "tunnel."

3. Tell the participants that they will be playing the "Cars" game. The object of the game is to move around the room without crashing into anything, including other cars. Participants in front will serve as "cars" and the people behind them will serve as "drivers," using their hands on the shoulders of the "cars" to steer them. The catch is that the cars have to keep their eyes closed while they are being driven. They cannot open their eyes at all and have to rely on the driver to keep them from crashing into something.

4. Tell participants to start their engines! After a few moments, ask pairs to switch places and let the "car" become the "driver." Allow everyone to have a chance to participate.

Asset-Building Teaching Points

Ask the group the following questions: How did it feel to be a "car" in this activity? Did you feel nervous about letting someone else guide you around the room with your eyes closed? What was it like to be a "driver"? Did you feel like you had to be especially cautious? How is this activity an example of our own lives and our experiences in community building? Sometimes it can be difficult to share with others what is precious to us. We wonder, "Will others care as much as I do?" and "Will they work to protect it?" This is what being an asset builder is all about. We have to be willing to let others share our tribulations as well as our triumphs.

Tip for Success

Depending on the size of the group and space available, you may want to only have two to four cars out of the parking lot at a time and let participants take turns.

Activity contributed by Jim Williams, Junction City, Kansas.

#41 ► Huddle Up!

Purpose: To energize participants during in-between times.

Suggested Group Size: 10 to 50.

Estimated Time: 10 to 12 minutes.

Materials Needed: None.

Directions

1. Ask participants to stand in an open or cleared area of the room. Explain to the group that when a number is called out they will assemble together or "Huddle Up" into groups of that size. (For example, "Two!" will result in people forming pairs.)

2. Call out a number. After groups are formed, give them a topic to discuss and a one- to two-minute time limit. (Groups can have a very general discussion such as a brief introduction or a more specific one, such as what brought them to the meeting or presentation.)

3. Call out another number and give groups a second assignment. This time, tie the question to the specific purpose of your gathering, such as "What would you most like to do for the youth in your community?" "How many of the youth in your community do you know by name?" "What types of activities and resources are available to youth in your community?" Give participants two minutes to answer; keep in mind that in this second grouping, there should be no more than two people from the first "huddle."

4. Repeat two or three more times if your schedule allows. Four to five "huddles" is usually the maximum to use before groups lose interest.

Asset-Building Teaching Points

It's amazing how much information you can learn about someone in just a matter of minutes. What are some of the things you learned about other participants in this activity? Did any of you have similar reasons for being here or things that you'd like to accomplish?

Tips for Success

Think about the sequence of questions you pose to the group. Use the questions you pose to move your meeting topic forward.

Activity contributed by Jim Williams, Junction City, Kansas.

Section 5

Wrap Things Up:
Closers and Reflections

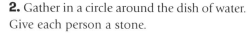

#42 ▶ Make a Ripple

Directions

1. At the end of the session, invite each participant to think of one thing he or she can do tomorrow that will help start ripples of change in her or his community or organization.

2. Gather in a circle around the dish of water. Give each person a stone.

3. Invite each participant to tell the one thing he or she will do to make ripples of change, and then toss her or his stone into the water.

4. After all have spoken, invite each participant to pick a stone out of the water to take as a reminder of the commitments made during this session.

Asset-Building Teaching Points

Every small effort we make to change our communities for the better makes an important ripple in asset building. The commitments that we've made today are important. Each one of us has a part in supporting and encouraging our youth. That should never be taken lightly.

Tips for Success

Be sure to have enough stones or coins for the number of participants attending. If your group is larger, form teams of 15–20, giving each team a basin of water.

Variations

Instead of stones you could use coins or tokens and call the activity "Small Treasures." You can ask participants to share one thing that makes them happy or one thing that they are looking forward to doing after the workshop, seminar, or presentation. Or use white beads or similar objects and call the activity "Pearls of Wisdom." Ask participants to share one "pearl" from the session that could have a ripple effect throughout the community.

#43 ▶ Asset Plan(e)s

Purpose: To help participants form a network to support each other's asset-building activities.

Suggested Group Size: At least 5, better with very large groups.

Estimated Time: 10 minutes.

Materials Needed: "Asset Plan(e)s" activity sheet from page 65 (one per person); pencils or pens.

Directions

1. Distribute activity sheets and invite participants, as they fill them out, to think about their own roles as asset builders.

2. Have participants fold their sheets into paper airplanes, helping each other as necessary.

3. Gather at one end of the room and fly all the planes to the other end.

4. Have participants pick up someone else's plane and read what is written.

Asset-Building Teaching Points

Do you know what allows a plane to glide in the air? The wings. The wings manipulate air pressure to "lift" the plane and keep it balanced. Sometimes, we need a "lift or a boost" from someone who knows what it's like to do the very important work that we do and keep us balanced. As we leave here today, let us make a commitment to contact the person listed on our paper airplane in some way and let them know that we support them.

Tip for Success

Copy the activity on brightly colored paper to add a festive tone.

Variation

"Affirmation Blizzard"—Participants form a circle and write one positive thing they would love to say about asset building on separate pieces of paper. Everyone then balls their pieces of paper up and creates a "blizzard" by throwing them into the center of the circle. Invite everyone to pick up an affirmation and read it. If there is time, participants can share them out loud with the group.

Asset Plan(e)s Activity Sheet

Name:_____

My action plan(e):

_____
_____
_____
_____
_____

Phone # or email address:_____

In the next six months, I will connect with a young person in this way:

_____
_____
_____
_____
_____
_____
_____

In the next six months, I will share the asset message in my community in this way:

_____
_____
_____
_____
_____
_____
_____

Purpose: To allow participants to think about assets creatively.

Suggested Group Size: At least 4.

Estimated Time: 10 to 12 minutes.

Materials Needed: Construction paper (enough for two sheets per team of four to eight); string; scissors.

Directions

1. Divide participants into teams of four to eight people.

2. Ask each team to create some room decoration that represents the value of youth, youth assets, their community, or some other designated topic. With their limited resources, each group creates a visual representation of the topic.

3. Display the decorations. If time permits, each group can describe its creation with the larger group.

Asset-Building Teaching Point

"How do these creations represent asset building?" Some responses might be: "We can be creative even though we have limited time and resources" or "There is something tangible and concrete that we can do to build assets!" (The creations can be displayed regularly if this is an ongoing team. Doing so establishes ownership of the team's space and an identity.)

Variation

Instead of construction paper, you could use popsicle sticks or toothpicks and glue.

Activity contributed by Marilyn Peplau, New Richmond, Wisconsin.

#45 ▶ Resource Scavenger Hunt

> **Purpose:** To introduce participants to useful tools and publications in a hands-on way.
>
> **Suggested Group Size:** Any size.
>
> **Estimated Time:** 12 to 15 minutes.
>
> **Materials Needed:** Index cards; copies of recent publications and tools on asset building that would be of interest and help to your audience.

Directions

1. For each resource you want to introduce, prepare an index card with these three parts:

- Title of resource;

- An identity/scenario for a small group that reflects one potential audience (examples: for the *Speaker's Kit,* "You are preparing to speak to business leaders"; for the *Tool Kit,* "You are on the planning team for a new community initiative"; for *What Kids Need to Succeed,* "You are part of a group addressing low scores on your youth survey"; for *Building Assets Together,* "You want to introduce assets to youth in your classroom"; and so on); and

- An assignment for the small group to complete that will get them into the actual resource (examples: Find three useful ideas to get your group started; choose key sections or ideas that you want to share with others; find sections that will help you answer tough questions from your community; choose three ideas to use with families).

2. Divide participants into groups of two or three and give each small group a resource and the prepared index card for it. Allow about 10 minutes for them to explore the resource and respond to the assignment.

3. Allow a minute or two for each small group to share something they have learned about the resource with the large group.

Asset-Building Teaching Points

Resources can make an important difference in spreading the asset-building message. A number of useful resources are available that specifically address the 40 developmental assets and their relevance in various parts of our communities. Other resources are highly relevant for people who are already building assets. This exercise was meant to give you an idea of what is available. The rest is up to you!

Tips for Success

Keep teams small—no more than three people—so that each person has a chance to actually see the resource. Make sure you have enough resources so that each small group has one to look through. Search Institute's catalog includes a number of resources that may be useful. In addition, many asset-building publications include bibliographies of helpful resources for asset builders.

Variations

If you have time, rotate resources and cards so that each group has a chance to look through several of them. If your time is limited, do not take time for small groups to share with the larger group.

#46 ▶ Summing It Up

Purpose: To allow participants to reflect on what they learned and how they can communicate that information to others.

Suggested Group Size: Any size.

Estimated Time: 10 minutes.

Materials Needed: None.

Asset-Building Teaching Points

What good is any information if we don't remember it? Who will benefit from it? Taking a moment to reflect on what we learned and then explaining that information to someone else is a great way to be sure that we retain what learned. When we head back to our community, we'll have that much more knowledge to share with others who need it.

Activity contributed by Marilyn Peplau,
New Richmond, Wisconsin

Directions

1. Ask each participant to find a partner.

2. One person in each pair plays the role of someone who has not attended the presentation or meeting and poses questions such as, "What did you learn?" The other summarizes what he or she experienced or felt about it.

3. Ask partners to switch roles. After each pair has had the opportunity to complete the activity, challenge all participants to share within 24 hours with someone who was not in attendance what they learned or gained during the presentation or meeting.

#47 ► Toasting to Assets

Directions

1. Tell participants that you would like everyone to join in a toast. Distribute the glasses or cups of sparkling cider or juice and ask everyone to form a circle. Offer a toast similar to this: "From now on, let each of us more intentionally try to build assets not only in the young people around us but in ourselves as well." Ask participants to make their own toasts.

2. Thank participants for attending.

Tips for Success

You may want to pour sparkling cider into glasses or cups before the toast begins. If you have time to prepare them, make your toast with root beer floats!

#48 ▶ All Hands On Deck

> **Purpose:** To help participants think about the roles they have in asset building.
>
> **Suggested Group Size:** Any size.
>
> **Estimated Time:** 10 to 12 minutes.
>
> **Materials Needed:** Colored or white paper; markers; pencils or pens.

Directions

1. Ask each participant to trace her or his dominant hand.

2. Instruct the participants to label each finger using the following criteria:

Thumb (so versatile)—a unique gift/ asset that you share with others;

Index finger (the pointer)—best information received today;

Middle finger (tall person)—a goal related to asset building that you have set for yourself;

Ring finger (where rings symbolize relationships)—a significant person in your lives with whom asset building occurs regularly;

Pinky finger—a word, cue, or mantra to remind you of today's presentation;

Palm—your "lifeline"; what keeps you going; your passion.

3. After completing the hand individually, participants shake hands and share any part of what they've created with each other. Ask for volunteers to share some of the comments as a closure.

Asset-Building Teaching Points

It takes all hands on deck to support our youth! Let's all make it a goal when we return to our communities to remember what we accomplished here today. Put your "hands" in a special place where you will see them on a regular basis, so that you might be reminded to use your hands, your feet, your minds, and, most important, your hearts to show a young person just how much you care about her or him. Try to do this as often as possible.

Variations

Instead of hands you could pass out skeleton or body outlines for participants to use in a similar way. For example, the "head" may be where the group would write what they learned, and the "heart" might be a good place to write what keeps them going in their efforts. Or, give participants the opportunity to link their hands as they post them on the wall to symbolize the benefits of working together and to reinforce the notion that "many hands make for a lighter load."

Activity contributed by Marilyn Peplau, New Richmond, Wisconsin.

#49 ▶ Group Review Game

Directions

1. Before the session, develop a list of 8 to 10 questions that review the key information you will be presenting at the workshop. Print them on chart paper or prepare them for overhead projection. Label each ball or other toy with masking tape and a letter for each group (to be able to tell them apart).

2. Use yarn or masking tape to mark a circle on the floor that is about 10 feet in diameter. Place an empty wastebasket or bucket in the center of the circle.

3. To play the game, divide participants into teams of five. Give each group a ball or other toss toy and tell them that group members will take turns being the "thrower."

4. Post questions one at a time. Each small group that wants to answer the question sends its "thrower" to the edge of the marked circle to try to get their ball into the wastebasket or bucket. Each group that gets its toy into the container gets to answer the question. Give one point to each team that answers correctly.

5. Repeat this process for each question you have prepared and give the winning team a round of applause at the end of the game.

Asset-Building Teaching Points

Here are some ideas for questions to use in this activity: What are the developmental assets? What are some ways that we can build them in young people? What are some of the ideas expressed by the youth in our group today?

Tip for Success

Make sure you have enough space for a big circle.

Variation

For more of a challenge, allow only the first two groups that get their toy into the container the opportunity to answer.

#50 ▶ Another Circle Game

Purpose: To close on a positive, upbeat note and to give participants ideas to think about. (This activity can serve as part II of Activity #6, "The Circle Game.")

Suggested Group Size: 14 to 40.

Estimated Time: 10 minutes.

Materials Needed: One index card for each person numbered consecutively (such as 1-15 with one number on each card); masking tape.

Directions

1. Ask participants to form a circle and distribute the numbered index cards, taking care to preserve the order. Ask each participant to tape the card to the floor in front of her or him and to remember the number.

2. Ask participants to spend a few minutes thinking about one important insight they received during the meeting or presentation. Give participants 2–3 minutes.

3. Instruct participants that, at your signal, each participant will break the circle, find a partner, say their name and number (on the index card), and share the insight they received. When each partner has shared, participants will return to the circle, but will now stand in the place where their sharing partner had been.

4. Process the activity by asking, "How did this circle game differ from the one we played at the beginning of the workshop?" (Everyone moved at once—we had a common focus; our movement was more intentional, with a specific direction; no one was left standing alone in the middle—we all had a role to play.)

Asset-Building Teaching Points

Conclude by saying something similar to the following: "The first game illustrated common elements in youth work, and the differences we just discussed reflect the importance of asset building. In some ways much of what we do will be the same, but the asset approach can add a developmental framework and an increased level of intentionality to the youth development process."

Adapted with permission from James Conway, *Integrating Assets into Congregations: A Curriculum for Trainers* (Minneapolis: Search Institute, 2000).

Hey, Presenters!

Do you have a great asset-building icebreaker, game, or activity that you would like to share with other communities across the country?

Here's your chance to *shine!*

The Search Institute Editorial staff is looking for good ideas to add to future publications similar to *Get Things Going!*

If you are interested in contributing your ideas, please send the following information to:

> Search Institute
> 615 First Avenue Northeast, Suite 125
> Minneapolis, MN 55413
> Fax: 612-692-5553
> www.search-institute.org

We will contact you soon to get the scoop!

Name: _____

Organization: _____

Email address: _____

Daytime telephone number:_____

Name of activity/idea: _____

Thanks so much for your time and interest!!!